Contents

Ich

heiße

die Taube

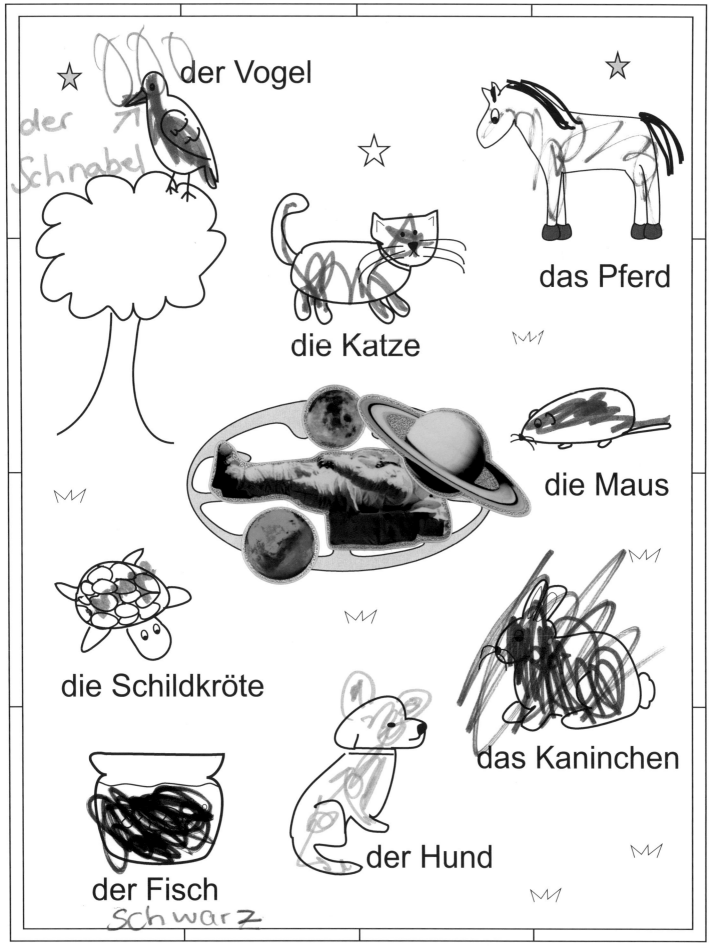

der Vogel

der Schnabel

das Pferd

die Katze

die Maus

die Schildkröte

das Kaninchen

der Fisch

der Hund

schwarz

1

Tiere (Animals)

Schreib das korrekte deutsche Wort zu jedem Bild:
(Write the correct German word under each picture:)

1) *der Fisch*

der Fisch

2) Der Kaninchen

3) den Pferd Pferd

4) der Hund

5) die Katze

6) der Vogel

7) die Maus

8) die Schildkröte

der Hund   der Fisch   der Vogel   die Katze   die Schildkröte   die Maus   das Pferd   das Kaninchen

Welches Tier ist das? (What animal is it?)

Schreib das korrekte deutsche Wort unter jedes Bild:
(Write the correct German word under each picture:)

1) *der Hund*

2) _____

3) _____

4) _____

5) _____

6) _____

7) _____

 der Hund   der Fisch   der Vogel   die Katze   die Schildkröte  die Maus das Pferd   das Kaninchen

3

Zählen macht Spaß! (Counting is fun!)

Zähle und notiere die richtige Anzahl auf Deutsch.
(Count and write the correct number in German.)

sieben ✎

_____ Hund**e**　　　　　_____ Fisch**e**

_____ Pferd**e**　　　　　_____ Mäus**e**

_____ V**ö**gel　　　　　　_____ Kaninchen

_____ Katz**e**n　　　　　_____ Schildkröt**e**n

1	2	3	4	5	6	7	8	9	10
eins	zwei	drei	vier	fünf	sechs	sieben	acht	neun	zehn

Hast du Haustiere? (Do you have a pet?)

name animals

| Ich heiße ….. My name is | Ich habe ….I have | und …and |

> Ich heiße Stefanie.
> Ich habe eine Katze.

> Ich heiße Peter.
> Ich habe einen Hund.

> Ich heiße Thomas.
> Ich habe ein Pferd.

> Ich heiße Sarah.
> Ich habe ein Kaninchen.

> Ich heiße Caroline.
> Ich habe einen Vogel.

> Ich heiße Benjamin.
> Ich habe einen Fisch und
> eine Schildkröte.

Beantworte die Fragen: (Answer the questions:)

1) Who has a horse? _____Thomas_____

2) Who has a dog? _____Peter_____

3) What pet does Stefanie have? _____eine Katze_____

4) What pet does Sarah have? _____ein Kaninchen_____

5) Who has two pets? _____Benjamin_____

6) Who ~~has a bird~~? *is crazy* _____Caroline_____

5

Welche Farbe haben sie? (What colour are they?)

Mal die Bilder in der richtigen Farbe an:
(Colour the pictures using the correct colour:)

rot = red	blau = blue	gelb = yellow	grün = green
grau = grey	weiß = white	schwarz = black	braun = brown

Der Vogel ist rot.

Die Schildkröte ist grün.

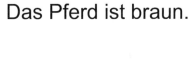

Das Pferd ist braun.

Die Maus ist weiß.

Die Katze ist schwarz.

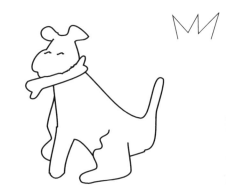

Der Hund ist braun.

Das Kaninchen ist grau.

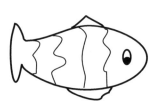

Der Fisch ist gelb.

Der Fisch ist blau.

Hast du Haustiere? (Do you have a pet?)

> Ich habe = I have   Ich hätte gern = I would like

Hallo!
Hast du Haustiere? Ich habe einen Fisch.
Der Fisch ist orange. Ich hätte gern einen Hund.
Bis bald!
    Peter

Hallo!
Ich habe eine Katze .
Die Katze ist schwarz.
Ich hätte gern ein Pferd.
    Bis bald!
        Stefanie

Hallo!
Ich habe eine Schildkröte.
Die Schildkröte ist braun.
Ich hätte gern ein Kaninchen.
Bis bald!
    Sarah

Füll die Tabelle aus! (Fill in the table)

	What pet does he/she have?	What colour is the pet?	What pet would he/she like to have?
Peter			
Stefanie			
Sarah			

7

Gitterrätsel (Word search)

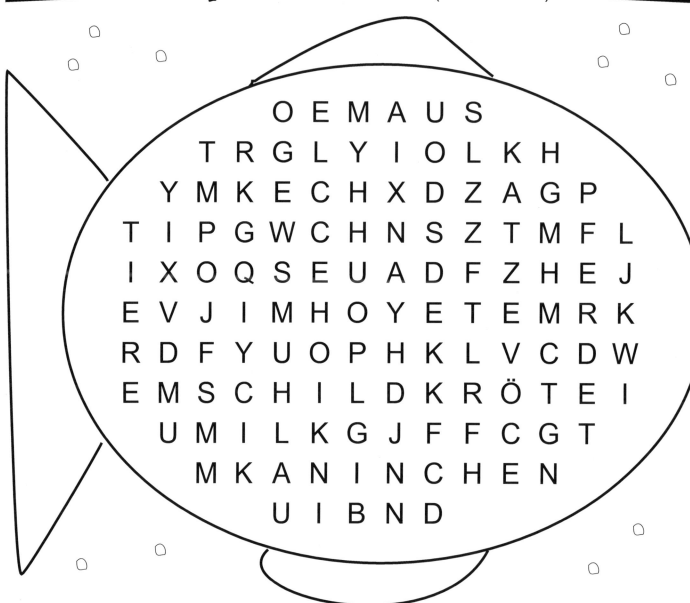

```
    O E M A U S
  T R G L Y I O L K H
Y M K E C H X D Z A G P
T I P G W C H N S Z T M F L
I X O Q S E U A D F Z H E J
E V J I M H O Y E T E M R K
R D F Y U O P H K L V C D W
E M S C H I L D K R Ö T E I
  U M I L K G J F F C G T
    M K A N I N C H E N
        U I B N D
```

Such die Wörter: (Look for the words:)

der Hund

der Fisch

die Schildkröte

die Maus

die Tiere

der Vogel

die Katze

das Pferd

das Kaninchen

In German there are three different ways of saying our word "the": der, die, das.
These words do not appear in the word search.

elf

zwölf

dreizehn

vierzehn

fünfzehn

sechzehn

Zahlen 11 - 20

siebzehn

achtzehn

neunzehn

zwanzig

Zahlen 1 - 20 (Numbers 11-20)

Trag die fehlenden Zahlen ein: (Fill in the missing numbers)

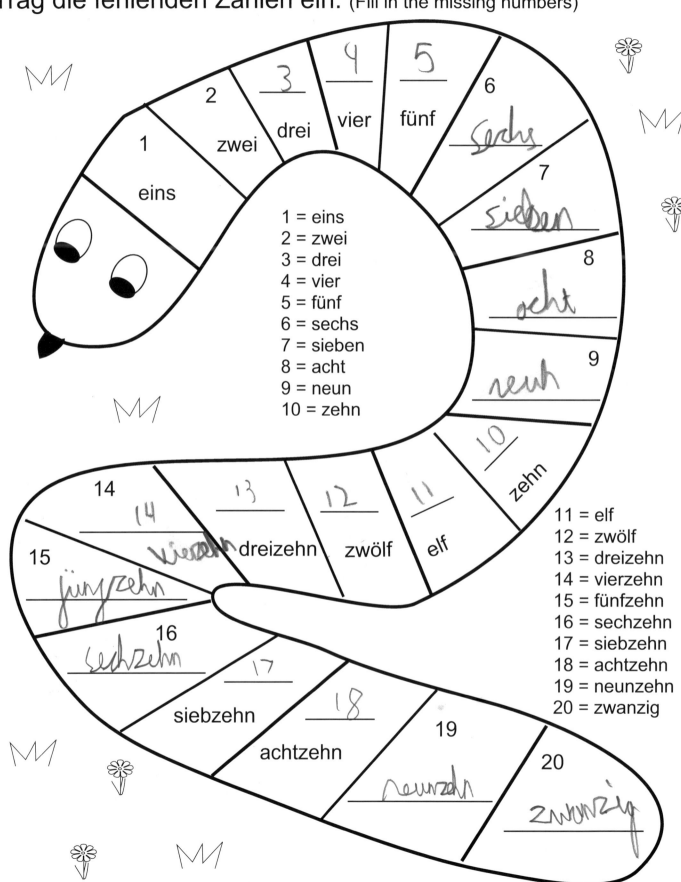

1 = eins
2 = zwei
3 = drei
4 = vier
5 = fünf
6 = sechs
7 = sieben
8 = acht
9 = neun
10 = zehn

11 = elf
12 = zwölf
13 = dreizehn
14 = vierzehn
15 = fünfzehn
16 = sechzehn
17 = siebzehn
18 = achtzehn
19 = neunzehn
20 = zwanzig

Zählen macht Spaß! (Counting is fun!)

Zähle und notiere die richtige Anzahl auf Deutsch.
(Count and write the correct number in German.)

a)
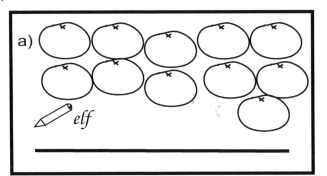
elf
_____

b)
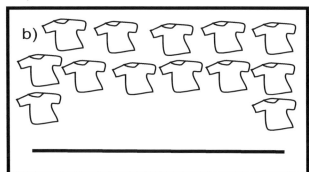
_____

c)
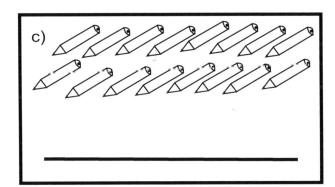
_____

d)
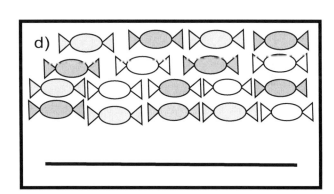
_____

e)
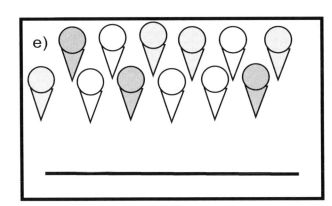
_____

f)
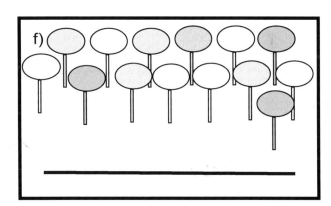
_____

g)
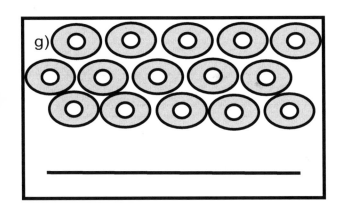
_____

h)
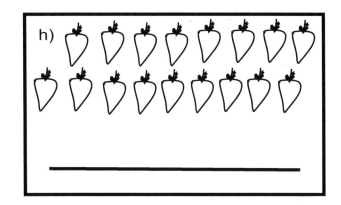
_____

11	12	13	14	15	16	17	18	19	20
elf	zwölf	dreizehn	vierzehn	fünfzehn	sechzehn	siebzehn	achtzehn	neunzehn	zwanzig

Zahlen 11 - 20

Welche Zahl ist das? (What number is it?)

l e f

elf
ely

c a h h z t e n

achtzehn

e r v e
z h n i

vierzehn

z n e h
e s h c

Sechzehn

f w z l ö

zwölf

w i a z z n g

zwanzig

z s i h e n e b

siebzehn

11	12	13	14	15	16	17	18	19	20
elf	zwölf	dreizehn	vierzehn	fünfzehn	sechzehn	siebzehn	achtzehn	neunzehn	zwanzig

Welche Farben haben die Roboter? ✗

(What colour are the robots?)

Mal die Roboter in der richtigen Farbe an: (Colour the robots in the correct colour:)

Roboter Nummer elf ist rot. (Robot number 11 is red)

Roboter Nummer vierzehn ist blau.

Roboter Nummer siebzehn ist rosa.

Roboter Nummer dreizehn ist gelb.

Roboter Nummer zwanzig ist grün.

Roboter Nummer sechzehn ist lila.

rot	red
blau	blue
rosa	pink
gelb	yellow
grün	green
lila	purple

11	12	13	14	15	16	17	18	19	20
elf	zwölf	dreizehn	vierzehn	fünfzehn	sechzehn	siebzehn	achtzehn	neunzehn	zwanzig

13

Lass uns rechnen! (Let's do the calculations!)

Schreib die Lösungen auf deutsch: (Write the answers in German)

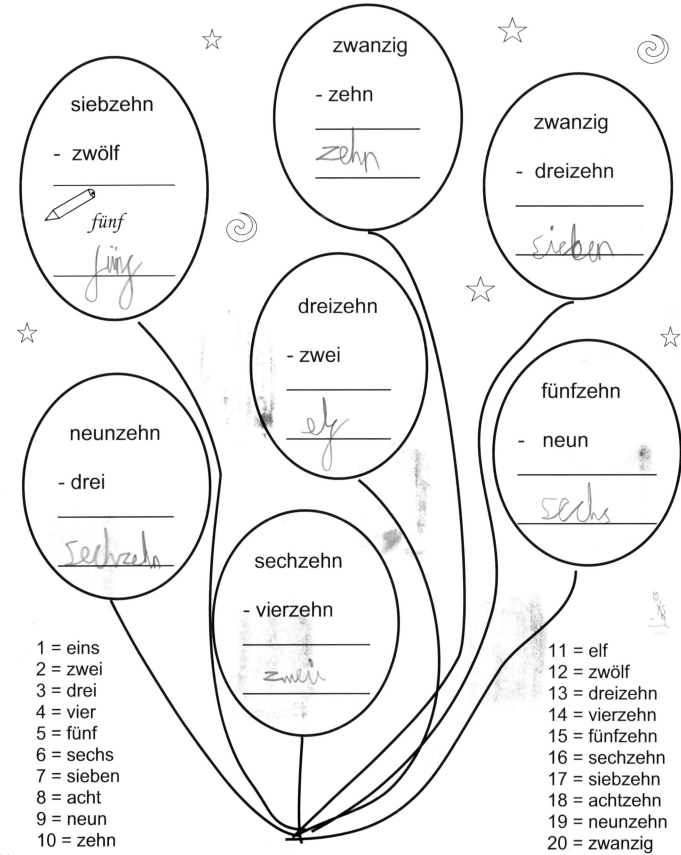

siebzehn

- zwölf

fünf

fünf

zwanzig

- zehn

zehn

zwanzig

- dreizehn

sieben

dreizehn

- zwei

elf

neunzehn

- drei

sechzehn

fünfzehn

- neun

sechs

sechzehn

- vierzehn

zwei

1 = eins
2 = zwei
3 = drei
4 = vier
5 = fünf
6 = sechs
7 = sieben
8 = acht
9 = neun
10 = zehn

11 = elf
12 = zwölf
13 = dreizehn
14 = vierzehn
15 = fünfzehn
16 = sechzehn
17 = siebzehn
18 = achtzehn
19 = neunzehn
20 = zwanzig

Gitterrätsel (Word search)

Such die Wörter (look for the words)

11 ELF	**14** VIERZEHN	**17** SIEBZEHN	**20** ZWANZIG
12 ZWÖLF	**15** FÜNFZEHN	**18** ACHTZEHN	
13 DREIZEHN	**16** SECHZEHN	**19** NEUNZEHN	

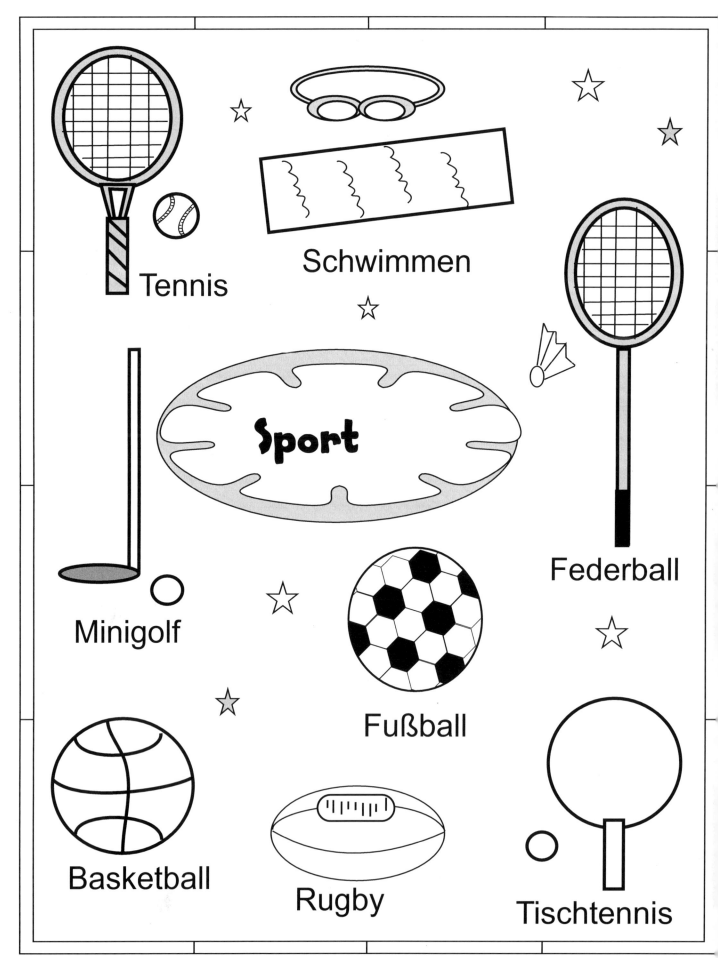

Tennis

Schwimmen

Sport

Federball

Minigolf

Fußball

Basketball

Rugby

Tischtennis

Sport

Schreib die Wörter ab und mal die Bilder ab:
(Copy the words and draw the pictures:)

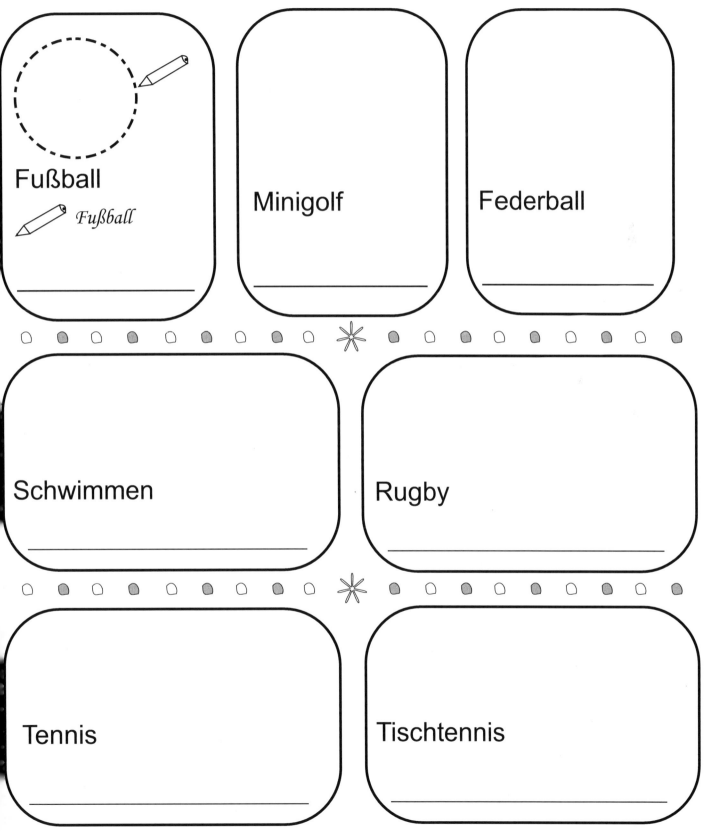

Fußball

Fußball

Minigolf

Federball

Schwimmen

Rugby

Tennis

Tischtennis

Ich mag Sport! (I like sports)

1) Lies die Briefe: (Read the letters:)

Hallo!
Ich heiße Peter.
Ich mag Fußball.
Fußball ist toll.
Bis bald!
      Peter

Hallo!
Ich heiße Sarah.
Ich mag Tennis
und Federball.
Bis bald!
      Sarah

Hallo!
Ich heiße Franz.
Ich mag Rugby
und Schwimmen.
Bis bald!
      Franz

2) Beantworte die Fragen: (Answer the questions:)

Sarah

a) Who likes rugby and swimming? _____

b) Who thinks football is great? (toll = great) _____

c) What sports does Sarah like? _____ and _____

3) Schreibe eine Antwort (Write a reply, saying your name and what sport you like. Use the following German phrases:)

Hallo = Hello

Ich heiße = my name is

Ich mag = I like

und = and

Bis bald = bye now

_____

_____

_____

_____

_____

Wochentage (Days of the week)

> Montag .... Monday
> Dienstag .... Tuesday
> Mittwoch .... Wednesday
> Donnerstag .... Thursday
> Freitag .... Friday
> Samstag .... Saturday
> Sonntag .... Sunday

Schreib das korrekte deutsche Wort neben das englische Wort:
(Write the correct German word next to the English word:)

Sonntag

a) Sunday _____

b) Friday _____

c) Monday _____

d) Saturday _____

e) Tuesday _____

f) Thursday _____

g) Wednesday _____

19

Montags spiele ich Tennis (On Monday I play tennis)

1) Lies den Brief: (Read the letter:)

Hallo!

Ich mag Sport.   Montags spiele ich Tennis.

Dienstags spiele ich Rugby. Rugby ist toll.

Mittwochs spiele ich Tischtennis.

Donnerstags spiele ich Basketball.

Freitags spiele ich Fußball.

Samstags spiele ich Federball.

Sonntags schwimme ich. Schwimmen ist toll.

Bis bald!

Stefanie

2) Beantworte die Fragen: (Answer the questions:)

On Wednesdays

a) What day does Stefanie play table tennis? _____

b) What day does she play badminton?   _____

c) What day does she swim?   _____

d) What does she play on Thursdays?   _____

e) What does she play on Mondays?   _____

f) What does she play on Fridays?   _____

g) What does she play on Tuesdays?   _____

Montags …. On Mondays   Dienstags … On Tuesdays   Mittwochs … On Wednesdays
Donnerstags … On Thursdays   Freitags.......... On Fridays
Samstags …… On Saturdays   Sonntags ……On Sundays

Welchen Sport magst du? (Which sports do you like?)

Imagine you meet a friendly German speaking alien who wants to know what various sports are like. Complete the sentences according to what you think each sport is like:

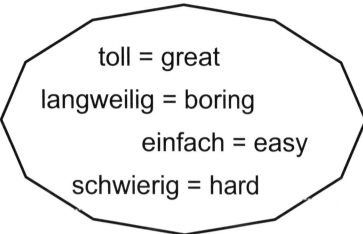

toll = great

langweilig = boring

einfach = easy

schwierig = hard

1) Wie ist Fußball?   Fußball ist _____ .

2) Wie ist Tennis?   Tennis ist _____ .

3) Wie ist Schwimmen?   Schwimmen ist _____ .

4) Wie ist Rugby?   Rugby ist _____ .

5) Wie ist Tischtennis?   Tischtennis ist _____ .

6) Wie ist Minigolf?   Minigolf ist _____ .

7) Wie ist Federball?   Federball ist _____ .

Gitterrätsel (Word search)

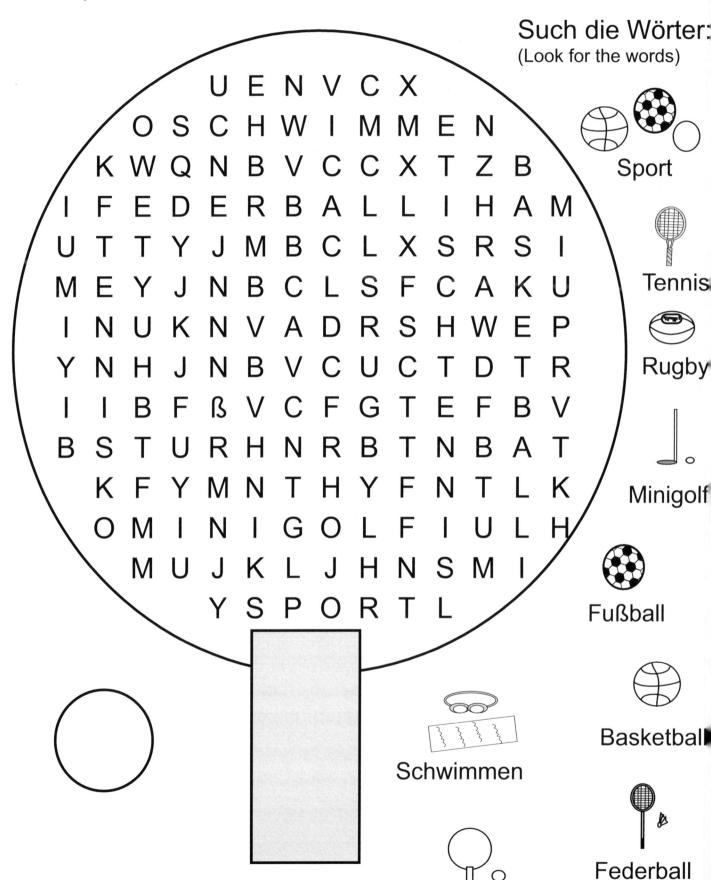

Such die Wörter:
(Look for the words)

U E N V C X
O S C H W I M M E N
K W Q N B V C C X T Z B
I F E D E R B A L L I H A M
U T T Y J M B C L X S R S I
M E Y J N B C L S F C A K U
I N U K N V A D R S H W E P
Y N H J N B V C U C T D T R
I I B F ß V C F G T E F B V
B S T U R H N R B T N B A T
K F Y M N T H Y F N T L K
O M I N I G O L F I U L H
M U J K L J H N S M I
Y S P O R T L

Sport

Tennis

Rugby

Minigolf

Fußball

Basketball

Schwimmen

Federball

Tischtennis

22

Es ist schön.

Es ist heiß.

Es ist sonnig.

Wetter

Es ist kalt.

Es regnet.

Es ist stürmisch.

Es schneit.

Das Wetter (The weather)

Verbinde die deutschen Wörter mit ihrem Bild:

(Draw a line between the German words and their picture:)

Es ist schön.

Es schneit.

Es regnet.

Es ist kalt.

Es ist sonnig.

Es ist heiß.

Es ist stürmisch.

24

Wie ist das Wetter? (What is the weather like?)

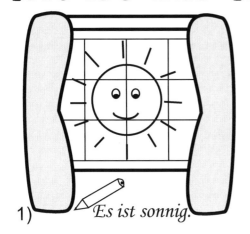

1) *Es ist sonnig.*

_____ .

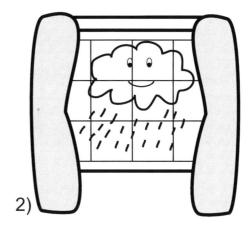

2) _____ .

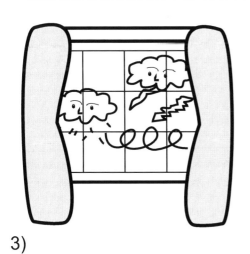

3) _____ .

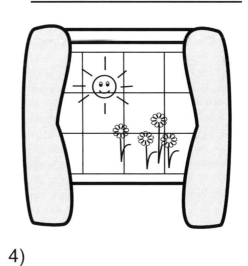

4) _____ .

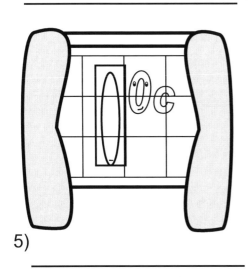

5) _____ .

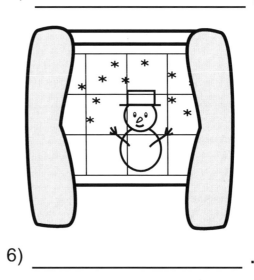

6) _____ .

Es ist stürmisch   Es regnet   Es ist sonnig   Es ist schön   Es ist heiß   Es ist kalt   Es schneit

Wie ist das Wetter? (What is the weather like?)

Mal die Bilder: (Draw the pictures:)

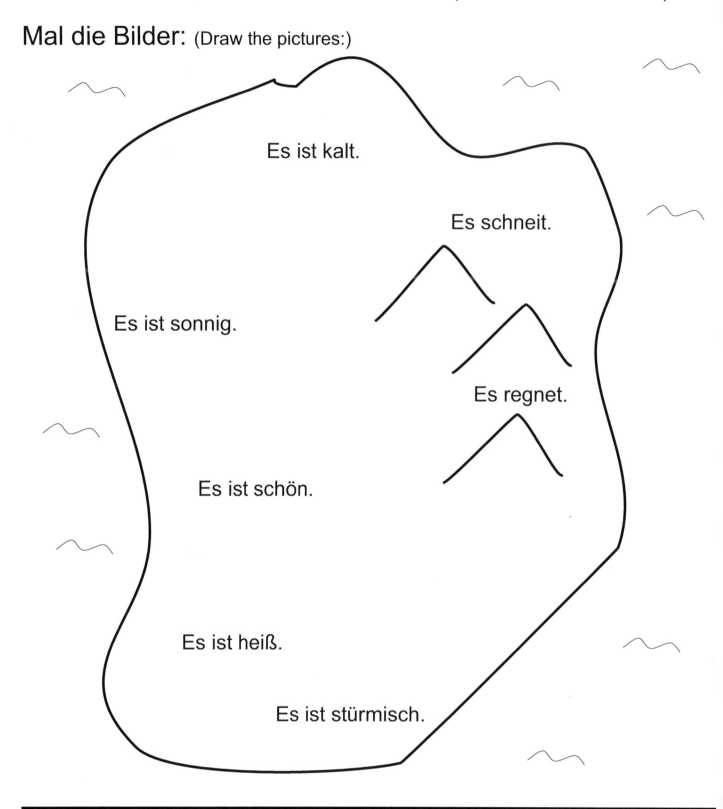

Es ist kalt.

Es schneit.

Es ist sonnig.

Es regnet.

Es ist schön.

Es ist heiß.

Es ist stürmisch.

Es ist stürmisch   Es regnet   Es ist sonnig   Es ist schön   Es ist heiß   Es ist kalt   Es schneit

Das Wetter (The weather)

Montag Es ist heiß.	**Samstag** Es ist kalt.
Dienstag Es ist sonnig.	
Mittwoch Es ist schön.	**Sonntag** Es schneit.
Donnerstag Es regnet.	
Freitag Es ist stürmisch.	

Beantworte die Fragen: (Answer the questions:)

Tuesday

1) What day is it sunny? _____

2) What day is it cold? _____

3) What day is it raining? _____

4) What day is it hot? _____

5) What day is it snowing? _____

6) What day is it stormy? _____

7) What day is it nice weather? _____

Montag	Monday
Dienstag	Tuesday
Mittwoch	Wednesday
Donnerstag ...	Thursday
Freitag.........	Friday
Samstag	Saturday
Sonntag	Sunday

Gitterrätsel (Word search)

Such die Wörter (Look for the words)

30 c **0 c**

HEIß   KALT

WETTER

SCHÖN   SONNIG

ES REGNET

ES SCHNEIT

STÜRMISCH

```
W  S  R  E  T  T  E  W  F  J
J  F  E  S  O  N  N  I  G  M  E
G  U  K  S  L  M  N  B  ß  H
H  D  I  C  M  K  F  I  G  K
D  T  Y  H  K  J  E  N  K  E
X  G  F  Ö  J  H  K  C  A  S
S  T  Y  N  J  K  L  M  L  C
C  B  H  G  F  F  C  F  T  S
X  S  T  Ü  R  M  I  S  C  H
S  Y  J  K  L  H  J  U  G  D
E  S  S  C  H  N  E  I  T  D
I  U  H  J  K  L  F  V  B  H
X  E  S  R  E  G  N  E  T  J
```

28

die Cola light

die Limonade

die Cola

Getränke

der Orangensaft

das Wasser

der Tee

der Kaffee

Welches Getränk ist das? (What drink is it?)

Schreib das korrekte deutsche Wort zu jedem Bild:
(Write the correct German word for each picture:)

der Orangensaft

1)

_____

2)

_____

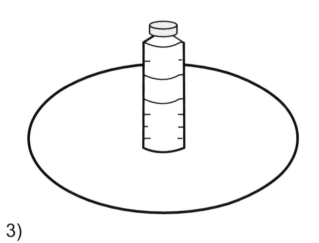

3)

_____

4)

_____

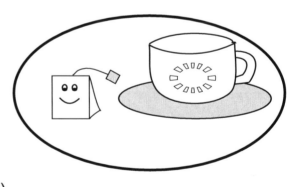

5)

_____

6)

_____

 die Cola   die Limonade   das Wasser   der Orangensaft   der Tee   der Kaffee

Malen macht Spaß! (Drawing is fun!)

Mal die richtige Anzahl der Dinge. (Draw the correct number of things):

1 = ein

2 = zwei

3 = drei

4 = vier

5 = fünf

a)

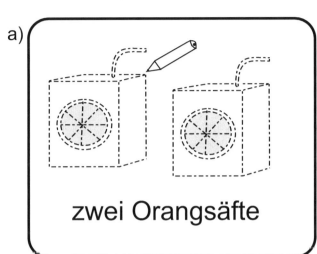

zwei Orangsäfte

b)

vier Tees

c)

fünf Limonaden

d)

drei Kaffees

e)

eine Cola light

▬ Ich hätte gern...., bitte (I would like..., please) ▬

In German, to ask for a drink use **Ich hätte gern**. This means I would like. After this, you need either **ein, einen** or **eine**:

Mineralwasser needs **ein** after Ich hätte gern ein Mineralwasser	Drinks using **einen** after Ich hätte gern : einen Orangensaft einen Tee einen Kaffee	Drinks using **eine** after Ich hätte gern : eine Cola eine Limonade eine Cola light

Bitte um die richtige Getränke: (Ask for the following drinks:)

a) *Ich hätte gern ein Mineralwasser, bitte.*

_____ .

b)

_____ .

c)

_____ .

d)

_____ .

e)

_____ .

Welche Getränke magst du? (What drinks do you like?)

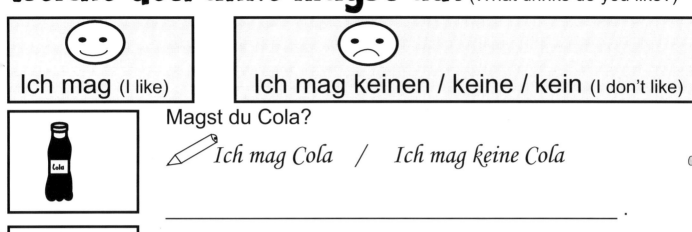

😊 Ich mag (I like)	☹️ Ich mag keinen / keine / kein (I don't like)

Magst du Cola?

Ich mag Cola / *Ich mag keine Cola*

_____ .

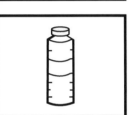

Magst du Limonade?
Ich mag Limonade / Ich mag keine Limonade

_____ .

Magst du Wasser?
Ich mag Wasser / Ich mag kein Wasser

_____ .

Magst du Kaffee?
Ich mag Kaffee / Ich mag keinen Kaffee

_____ .

Magst du Tee?
Ich mag Tee / Ich mag keinen Tee

_____ .

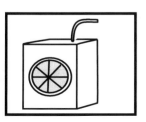

Magst du Cola light?
Ich mag Cola light / Ich mag keine Cola light

_____ .

Magst du Orangensaft?
Ich mag Orangensaft / Ich mag keinen Orangensaft

_____ .

Gitterrätsel (Word search)

```
M I N E R A L W A S S E R
J K L M N B J U G J L U Y
T O R A N G E N S A F T H
D G J K L C O J G G V C R
G L K C O L A L I G H T J
I I N M N U J K G B V F I
  M U J K E T E X Z D E
  O U K E N E B V C V X
  N U T J F K B Z O C R
  A K A F U X L Z L R M
  D D A J L U X G A T Y
  E K U K L Z N O R A N
  O R G E T R Ä N K E I
```

Such die Wörter:
(Look for the words)

 das **Mineralwasser**   der **Tee**

 die **Cola**   die **Limonade**   der **Kaffee**

 die **Cola light**   der **Orangensaft**   die **Getränke**

In German there are three different ways of saying our word "the": der, die, das.
These words do not appear in the word search.

a room = Zimmer

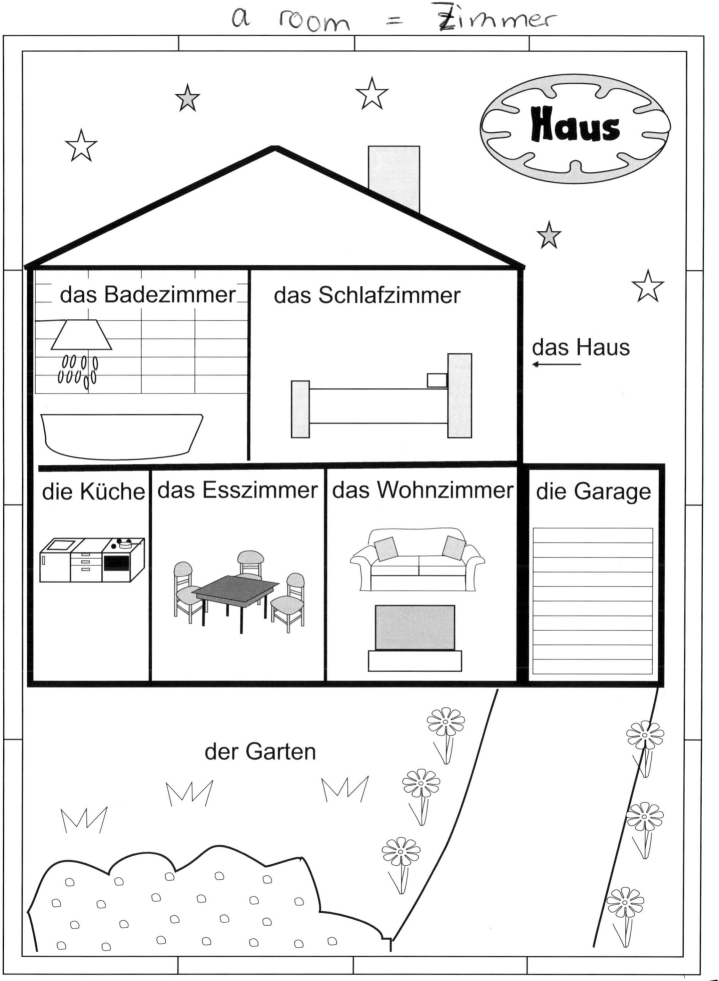

Haus

das Badezimmer

das Schlafzimmer

das Haus ←

die Küche

das Esszimmer

das Wohnzimmer

die Garage

der Garten

35

Das Haus (The house)

Schreib die Wörter ab und mal die Bilder ab:
(Copy the words and draw the pictures:)

 das Haus

das Haus

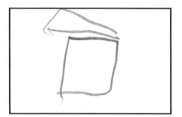

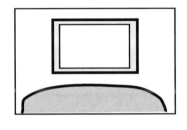 das Wohnzimmer

das Wohnzimmer

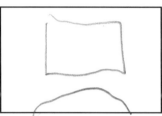

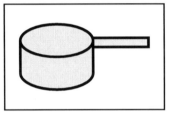 die Küche

die Küche

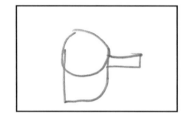

 das Esszimmer

das Esszimmer

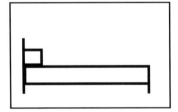 das Schlafzimmer

das Schlafzimmer

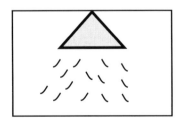 das Badezimmer

das Badezimmer

 der Garten

der Garten

Das Haus (The house)

Verbinde die deutschen Wörter mit ihrer englischen Bedeutung.

(Draw a line from the German words to their English meaning)

das Esszimmer

living room

die Garage

dining room

garage

das Wohnzimmer

das Badezimmer

der Garten

bedroom

kitchen

bathroom

Garden

die Küche

das Schlafzimmer

das Wohnzimmer = living room   die Küche = kitchen

das Badezimmer = bathroom   das Esszimmer = dining room

das Schlafzimmer = bedroom   die Garage = garage   der Garten = garden

37

Welche Farbe ist das? (What colour is it?)

1) Benutze die richtigen Farben: (Colour in using the correct colours:)

Das Wohnzimmer ist rot. (The living room is red)

Das Esszimmer ist gelb.

Die Küche ist grau.

Das Schlafzimmer ist lila.

Das Badezimmer ist blau.

Der Garten ist grün.

Die Garage ist weiß.

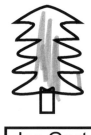

das Schlafzimmer | das Badezimmer

der Garten | die Garage | die Küche | das Esszimmer | das Wohnzimmer

2) Welche Farbe ist das? (What colour is it?)

a) The bedroom is _____ .

b) The living room is _____ .

c) The garage is _____ .

d) The dining room is _____ .

e) The kitchen is _____ .

f) The garden is _____ .

g) The bathroom is_____ .

| rot = red | gelb = yellow | grau = grey | lila = purple |
| blau = blue | grün = green | weiß = white | |

38

Wo sind die Tiere? 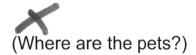 (Where are the pets?)

Peter isn't sure where all his pets are. Look at the plan of a bungalow, and where the animals are:

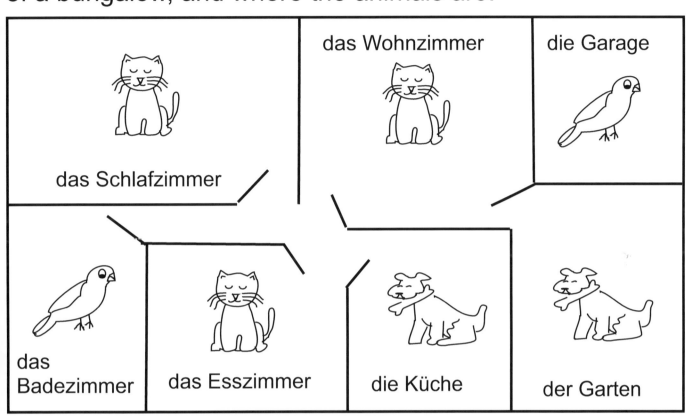

das Schlafzimmer

das Wohnzimmer

die Garage

das Badezimmer

das Esszimmer

die Küche

der Garten

Lies die Sätze. (Read the sentences.)
Sind sie richtig oder falsch?: (Are they true or false?)

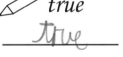 *true*

1) Eine Katze ist im Wohnzimmer. _____*true*_____ (A cat is in the living room.)

2) Ein Hund ist in der Küche. _____*true*_____ (A dog is in the kitchen.)

3) Ein Vogel ist im Esszimmer. _____*false*_____

4) Ein Hund ist im Schlafzimmer. _____*false*_____

5) Ein Vogel ist im Badezimmer. _____*true*_____

6) Eine Katze ist in der Garage. _____*false*_____

7) Ein Hund ist im Garten. _____*true*_____

eine Katze

ein Hund

ein Vogel

Gitterrätsel

(Word search)

B	E	W	O	H	N	Z	I	M	M	E	R
A	F	G	X	S	R	N	T	C	R	V	E
D	U	Z	U	M	E	R	H	E	I	G	M
E	M	A	K	T	Z	I	M	Y	N	A	M
Z	H	E	R	M	B	M	U	K	M	R	K
I	B	A	Z	U	I	M	H	Ü	V	A	D
M	G	F	G	Z	N	J	K	C	L	G	N
M	X	R	S	T	K	M	N	H	J	E	K
E	E	S	N	M	I	K	L	E	M	N	B
R	E	J	K	I	M	M	E	R	D	S	E
S	C	H	L	A	F	Z	I	M	M	E	R

Such die Wörter (look for the words)

 das **Haus**   die **Küche**   das **Wohnzimmer**   das **Esszimmer**

 das **Badezimmer**   das **Schlafzimmer**   die **Garage**   der **Garten**

In German there are three different ways of saying our word "the": der, die, das.
These words do not appear in the word search.

German	English	German	English
acht	eight	die Küche	the kitchen
achtzehn	eighteen	langweilig	boring
das Badezimmer	the bathroom	die Limonade	the lemonade
Basketball	basketball	Limonaden	lemonades
Bis bald	Bye now	Magst du....?	Do you like....?
bitte	please	die Maus	the mouse
blau	blue	Mäuse	mice
braun	brown	Minigolf	mini-golf
die Cola	the coke	Mittwoch	Wednesday
die Cola light	the diet coke	Montag	Monday
Dienstag	Tuesday	neun	nine
Donnerstag	Thursday	neunzehn	nineteen
drei	three	orange	orange
dreizehn	thirteen	der Orangensaft	the orange juice
einfach	easy	Orangensäfte	orange juices
eins	one	das Pferd	the horse
elf	eleven	Pferde	horses
Es ist heiß	It's hot	rot	red
Es Ist kalt	It's cold	Rugby	rugby
Es ist schön	It's nice weather	Samstag	Saturday
Es ist sonnig	It's sunny	die Schildkröte	the tortoise
Es ist stürmisch	It's stormy	Schildkröten	tortoises
Es regnet	It's raining	das Schlafzimmer	the bedroom
Es schneit	It's snowing	schwarz	black
das Esszimmer	the dining room	schwierig	difficult
Federball	badminton	das Schwimmen	swimming
der Fisch	the fish	sechs	six
Fische	fishes	sechzehn	sixteen
Freitag	Friday	sieben	seven
fünf	five	siebzehn	seventeen
fünfzehn	fifteen	Sonntag	Sunday
Fußball	football	der Tee	the tea
die Garage	the garage	Tees	teas
der Garten	the garden	Tennis	tennis
gelb	yellow	die Tiere	the animals
die Getränke	the drinks	Tischtennis	table tennis
grau	grey	toll	great
grün	green	und	and
hallo	hello	vier	four
Hast du..... ?	Do you have....?	vierzehn	fourteen
das Haus	the house	der Vogel	the bird
der Hund	the dog	Vögel	birds
Hunde	dogs	das Wasser	the water
Ich habe ….	I have	weiß	white
Ich hätte gern	I would like	das Wetter	the weather
Ich heiße ….	My name is …	die Wochentage	the days of the week
Ich mag	I like	das Wohnzimmer	the living room
Ich spiele	I play	die Zahlen	the numbers
der Kaffee	the coffee	zehn	ten
Kaffees	coffees	zwanzig	twenty

41

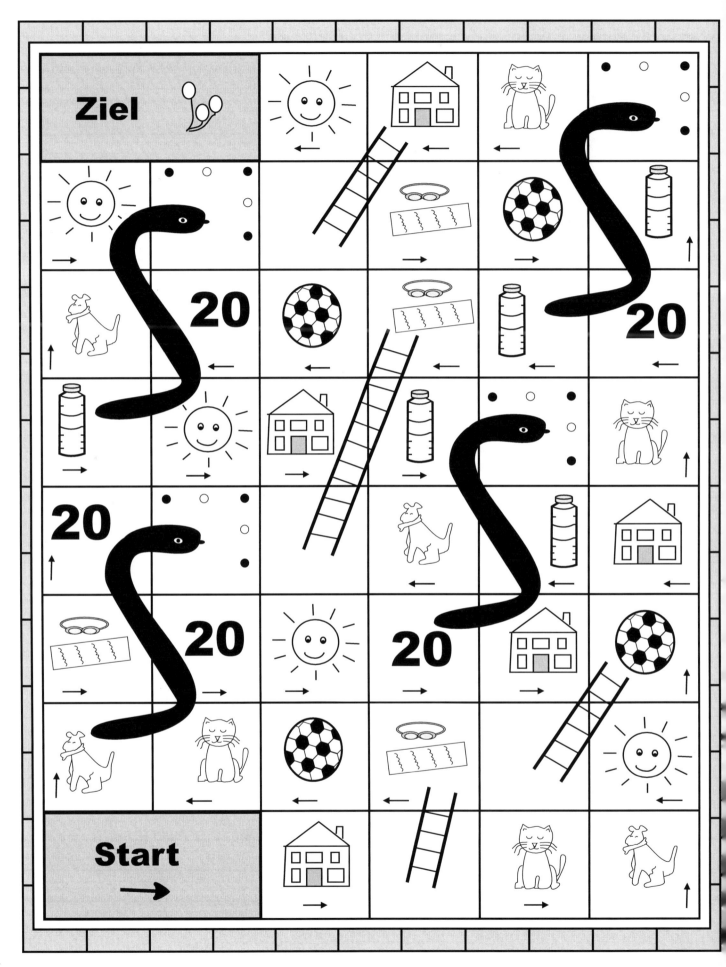

Snakes & ladders game

For this game, you will need a dice and a counter for each player. The counters could be rubbers, cubes or you could make your own on pieces of paper.

How to play

Place your counter at Start, roll the dice and count that number of squares.

If the final square has the bottom of the ladder in it go up it, or if it has the head of a snake go down it.

Say the word for the picture you land on in German.

Take turns to roll the dice. To win, arrive first at Ziel.

die Katze
(the cat)

der Hund
(the dog)

das Wasser
(the water)

das Haus
(the house)

Schwimmen
(swimming)

Fußball
(football)

20

zwanzig
(twenty)

Es ist sonnig.
(it's sunny.)

Games are a fun way to learn a foreign language! If you like games you could try the book: German Word Games - Cool Kids Speak German

Answers

Page 2

1) der Fisch
2) das Kaninchen
3) das Pferd
4) der Hund
5) die Katze
6) der Vogel
7) die Maus
8) die Schildkröte

Page 3

1) der Hund
2) der Vogel
3) die Katze
4) das Pferd
5) das Kanichen
6) die Maus
7) die Schildkröte

Page 4

sieben Hunde
vier Pferde
fünf Vögel
drei Katzen

drei Fische
zwei Mäuse
acht Kaninchen
vier Schildkröten

Page 5

1) Thomas
2) Peter
3) a cat
4) a rabbit
5) Benjamin
6) Caroline

Page 6

The horse is brown.
The bird is red.
The tortoise is green.
The rabbit is grey.
The cat is black.
The mouse is white.
The dog is brown.
The fish is yellow.
The fish is blue.

Page 7

	What pet does he/she have?	What colour is the pet?	What would he/she like?
Peter	a fish	orange	a dog
Sefanie	a cat	black	a horse
Sarah	a tortoise	brown	a rabbit

Page 8

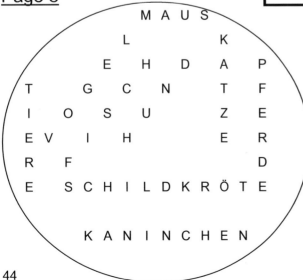

Page 10

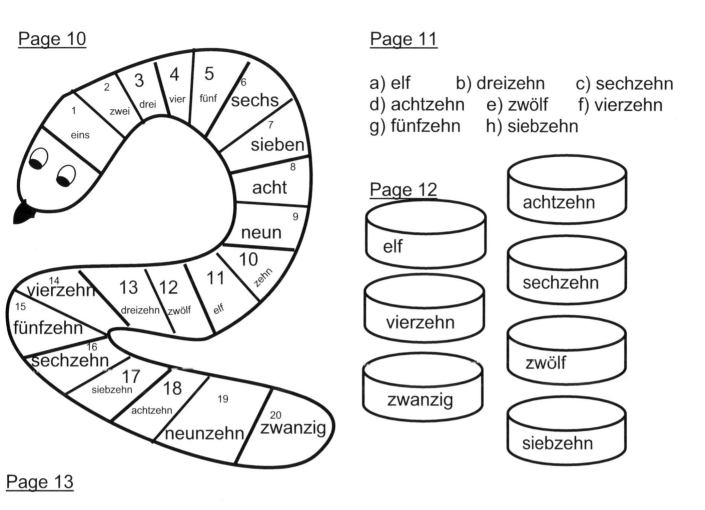

Page 11

a) elf   b) dreizehn   c) sechzehn
d) achtzehn   e) zwölf   f) vierzehn
g) fünfzehn   h) siebzehn

Page 12

elf

vierzehn

zwanzig

achtzehn

sechzehn

zwölf

siebzehn

Page 13

The robots should be coloured as follows:
Robot number 11 is red.   Robot number 17 is pink.   Robot number 20 is green.
Robot number 14 is blue.   Robot number 13 is yellow.   Robot number 16 is purple.

Page 14

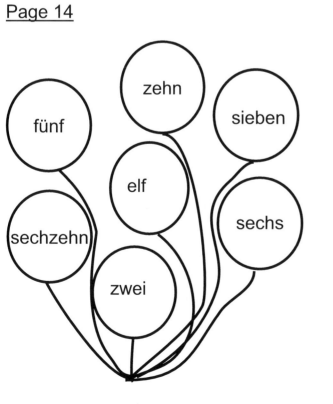

Page 15

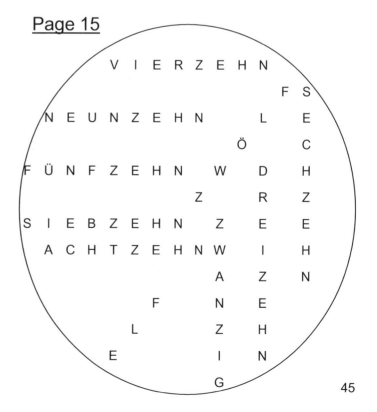

45

<u>Page 17</u>

A picture should be drawn the following, and the German words should be copied:
Fußball = football   Minigolf = Mini-golf   Federball = badminton
Schwimmen = swimming   Rugby = rugby   Tennis = tennis   Tischtennis = table tennis
<u>Page 18</u>

2a) Franz   b) Peter   c) tennis and badminton

3) The phrases should be in the following order, and completed:
Hallo,
Ich heiße ......,
Ich mag .... und ....
Bis bald!

<u>Page 19</u>

a) Sonntag   b) Freitag   c) Montag   d) Samstag   e) Dienstag
f) Donnerstag   g) Mittwoch

<u>Page 20</u>

1) On Wednesdays   2) On Saturdays   3) On Sundays   4) Basketball
5) Tennis   6) Football   7) Rugby

<u>Page 21</u>

The sentences should be completed with either toll, langweilig, einfach or schwierig
(Depending on what you think about the sport).

<u>Page 22</u>

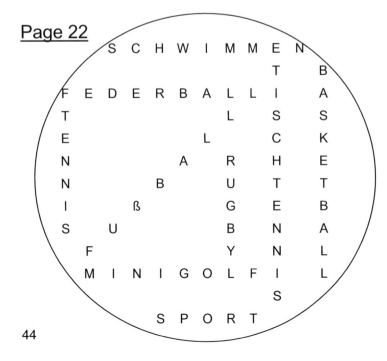

<u>Page 24</u>

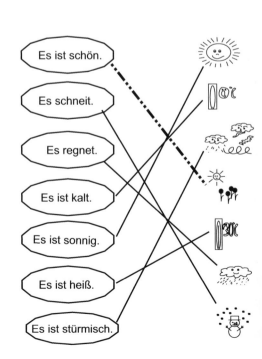

Es ist schön.
Es schneit.
Es regnet.
Es ist kalt.
Es ist sonnig.
Es ist heiß.
Es ist stürmisch.

44

Page 25

1) Es ist sonnig.   2) Es regnet.   3) Es ist stürmisch.   4) Es ist schön.
5) Es ist kalt.   6) Es schneit.

Page 26

Es ist kalt

Es schneit

Es ist sonnig

Es regnet

Es ist schön

Es ist heiß

Es ist stürmisch

Page 27

1) Tuesday
2) Saturday
3) Thursday
4) Monday
5) Sunday
6) Friday
7) Wednesday

Page 28

R E T T E W
S O N N I G
S ß
C I
H E K
Ö H A L
N T
S T Ü R M I S C H
E S S C H N E I T
E S R E G N E T

Page 30

1) der Orangensaft   2) die Cola   3) das Wasser   4) die Limonade
5) der Kaffee   6) der Tee

Page 31

The following should be drawn:
a) 2 orange juices   b) 4 teas   c) 5 lemonades   d) 3 coffees   e) 1 diet coke

Page 32

a) Ich hätte gern ein Mineralwasser, bitte.   b) Ich hätte gern eine Cola light, bitte.
c) Ich hätte gern einen Orangensaft, bitte.   d) Ich hätte gern einen Tee, bitte.
e) Ich hätte gern eine Limonade, bitte

Page 33

If you like the drink write: If you don't like the drink write:
Ich mag Cola   Ich mag keine Cola
Ich mag Limonade   Ich mag keine Limonade
Ich mag Wasser   Ich mag kein Wasser
Ich mag Kaffee   Ich mag keinen Kaffee
Ich mag Tee   Ich mag keinen Tee
Ich mag Cola light   Ich mag keine Cola light
Ich mag Orangensaft   Ich mag keinen Orangensaft

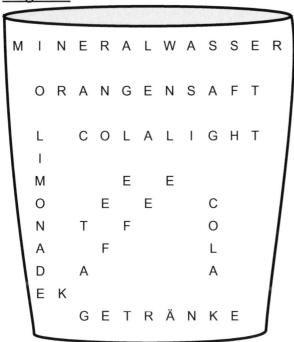

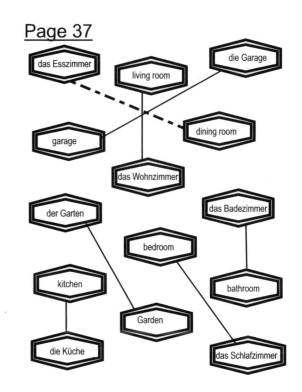

Page 38

1) The rooms in the house should be coloured as follows:

The living room is red.   The dining room is yellow.   The kitchen is grey.
The bedroom is purple.   The bathroom is blue.   The garden is green.
The garage is white.

2a) purple   b) red   c) white   d) yellow   e) grey   f) green   g) blue

Page 39

1) true
2) true
3) false
4) false
5) true
6) true
7) true

Page 40

B		W	O	H	N	Z		I	M	M		E	R
A				S		N				R			
D			U		E				E		G		
E		A		T			M				A		
Z	H		R			M		K			R		
I		A			I			Ü			A		
M	G			Z				C			G		
M			S					H			E		
E		S						E					
R	E												
S	C	H	L	A	F	Z	I	M	M		E	R	

First 100 Words In German Coloring Book - Cool Kids Speak German by Joanne Leyland

The 100 German words in this brilliant book include a marvellous mix of favourite children's characters (for example a fairy, a dragon, a mermaid, a dinosaur or a unicorn) and useful German words like some food, transport, animals, toys and clothes.

The 30 delightful pages all have borders and are single sided. On each page there are 3 or 4 German words, making a total of 100 German words throughout the whole book. Once completed this will be a lovely book to refer back to. Ideal for 7 - 11 year olds.

ISBN 9781914159558

---

40 German Word Searches Cool Kids Speak German by Joanne Leyland
Complete with vocabulary lists & answers. Let's make learning German fun!

With 40 exciting topics, this book is ideal to help learn or revise useful German vocabulary. Throughout the book the word searches appear in fun shapes and pictures accompany the German words so that each word search can be a meaningful learning activity. Ideal for children ages 7 - 11.

ISBN 9781914159541. The topics in this great book include:

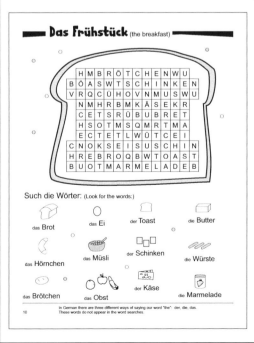

der Bauernhof (the farm)
die Begrüßungen (greetings)
der Campingplatz (the campsite)
das Eis (the ice creams)
das Essen (the food)
die Familie (the family)
die Farben (the colours)
das Federmäppchen (pencil case)
die Freizeit (free time/leisure)
das Frühstück (the breakfast)
der Garten (the garden)
mein Geburtstag (my birthday)
das Gemüse (the vegetables)
die Geschenke (the presents)
die Getränke (the drinks)
das Haus (the house)
das Hotel (the hotel)
die Kleidung (the clothes)
der Kopf (the head)
der Körper (the body)

die Möbel (the furniture)
die Monate (the months)
die Musik (the music)
der Nachtisch (the dessert)
das Obst (the fruit)
Ostern (Easter)
das Picknick (the picnic)
die Schulfächer (school subjects)
die Souvenirs (the souvenirs)
die Spielsachen (the toys)
der Sport (the sport)
die Stadt (the town / city)
der Strand (the beach)
die Tiere (the animals)
die Transportmittel (transport)
die Verben (the verbs)
das Wetter (the weather)
die Wochentage (tdays)
die Zahlen (the numbers)
der Zoo (the zoo)

Also available by Joanne Leyland:

French
Young Cool Kids Learn French
First Words In French Teacher's Resource Book
Cool Kids Speak French (books 1, 2 & 3)
French Word Games - Cool Kids Speak French
40 French Word Searches Cool Kids Speak French
Photocopiable Games For Teaching French
First 100 Words In French Coloring Book Cool Kids Speak French
French at Christmas time
On Holiday In France Cool Kids Speak French
Cool Kids Do Maths In French
Un Alien Sur La Terre
Le Singe Qui Change De Couleur
Tu As Un Animal?

Italian
Young Cool Kids Learn Italian
Cool Kids Speak Italian (books 1, 2 & 3)
Italian Word Games - Cool Kids Speak Italian
40 Italian Word Searches Cool Kids Speak Italian
First 100 Words In Italian Coloring Book Cool Kids Speak Italian
On Holiday In Italy Cool Kids Speak Italian
Un Alieno Sulla Terra
La Scimmia Che Cambia Colore
Hai Un Animale Domestico?

German
Young Cool Kids Learn German
Cool Kids Speak German (books 1, 2 & 3)
German Word Games - Cool Kids Speak German
40 German Word Searches Cool Kids Speak German
First 100 Words In German Coloring Book Cool Kids Speak German

Spanish
Young Cool Kids Learn Spanish
First Words In Spanish Teacher's Resource Book
Cool Kids Speak Spanish (books 1, 2 & 3)
Spanish Word Games - Cool Kids Speak Spanish
40 Spanish Word Searches Cool Kids Speak Spanish
Photocopiable Games For Teaching Spanish
First 100 Words In Spanish Coloring Book Cool Kids Speak Spanish
Spanish at Christmas time
On Holiday In Spain Cool Kids Speak Spanish
Cool Kids Do Maths In Spanish
Un Extraterrestre En La Tierra
El Mono Que Cambia De Color
Seis Mascotas Maravillosas

English as a foreign language
Cool Kids Speak English (books 1 & 2)
First Words In English - 100 Words To Colour & Learn

The word search editions have 40 topics in each book. The word searches are in fun shapes. Pictures accompany the words to find.

The first 100 words colouring book editions have 3 or 4 words per page, and are ideal for those who like to colour as they learn.

The stories in a foreign language have an English translation at the back.

If you like games, you could try the word game editions.

The holiday editions have essential words & phrases in part 1. And in part 2 there are challenges to use these words whilst away.

For more information on the books available, and different ways of learning a foreign language go to https://learnforeignwords.com

Printed in Great Britain
by Amazon

78685699R00032